Praise for *A Moth Fel...*

'If there was a way to meet the u...
this book of poetry would be it,
Kim Rashidi, Author of *Fortu...*

'This book is pure love for life seen through the light that shines
from the moon, that the moth longs for. Flor Ana is truly one of th
most beautiful poets in this lifetime and brings tears to my eyes. Sh
continues to connect with the reader in yet another stunning poetr
book,"
Kendall Hope, Author of *Pockets of Lavender: A Poetry Collection*

'With *A Moth Fell In Love With The Moon*, Flor Ana reminds th
reader of the simple joys of life, asking them to live in the present an
appreciate what they have, as the world is made of beautiful thing
Ana explores questions of purpose and satisfaction, with reflection
on human existence through accessible and modern poetic works. T
read this collection is to briefly hold the moon in your hands,"
Salem Paige, Author of *Take My Bleeding Heart*

'Ethereal is the only way to describe this collection. With an abur
dance of warmth and a loving nod to literature, Flor Ana provides
flame of awe and beauty for the reader to hold near,"
Cheyenne Raine, Author of *Maroon Daydreams*

A Moth Fell In Love With The Moon is a manifesto to openin
your eyes to the world around you with gratitude and hope. Thi
collection of poetry is for anyone looking to be reminded that ther
s beauty in everything the universe has brought in one's path. Flo
Ana is a phenomenal poet that all levels of readers will find easy t
connect with,"
Erin Flanagan, Author of *Haikus To Irish Tunes*

"Much like the moth and moon go through their phases, Flor takes us through the perennial ups and downs of being human. Some poems are sweet and others are spicy. Some poems are deep and others wrap you up in simple childlike wonder. If you're an introspective nature-lover, this book is for you."

- Joey Doherty, Author of *Subtle Medicine*

A MOTH FELL IN LOVE WITH THE MOON

(POEMS)

FLOR ANA

Edited by Athena Edwards & Kim Rashidi

1st Edition | 01
Paperback ISBN: 979-8-9869891-5-0

First Published March 2023

For inquiries and bulk orders, please email:
indieearthpublishinghouse@gmail.com

Indie Earth Publishing Inc.
| Miami, FL |

INDIE EARTH
PUBLISHING

Other works by Flor Ana

Perspective (and other poems) (2021)

The Language of Fungi & Flowers (2021)

Nourish Your Temple: Self-Love & Care Poetry (2022)

Featured works

Stories From The Forest:
10 Stories of Nature, Love, Loss, and Life
(Indie Earth Publishing, 2021)

The Spell Jar: Poetry For The Modern Witch
(Indie Earth Publishing, 2022)

Love Letters to the 305
(Indie Earth Publishing, 2023)

Saccharine Anthology
(Ampersand Press, 2023)

Listen to the
A Moth Fell In Love With The Moon
Auditory Experience

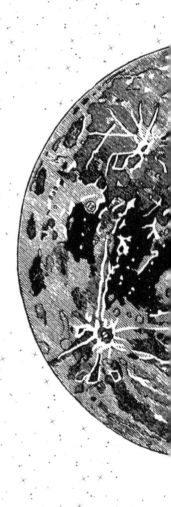

A MOTH FELL IN LOVE WITH THE MOON

WITH THE MOON

(POEMS)

For those who look at the moon
and long to kiss its craters...

{New Beginnings}

New Moon

When I Open My Eyes

if eyes are the window to the soul,
when i open mine,
i hope you see the love
that pours out through my veins.
the lust for life—

                for nature—

that keeps me sane.
i hope you see the magic
that emits itself effortlessly,
the whispers of words
escaping my tongue,
my lips,
the emotion that
flows through the strokes of my pen.
i hope you see
the love beyond the pain,
the laughter beyond the sorrow.
i hope you see all of me,
in all todays and all tomorrows.
i hope you see
my humanness, as well as my flaws—

                the galaxy, the ether—

i hope you see it all.

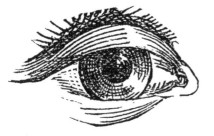
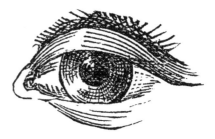

I eat poetry for breakfast

i eat poetry for breakfast,
each letter a piece of cereal
that i devour
with almond milk or alliteration.

sometimes,
i'll have poetry as a snack.
a little rhyme to satisfy my tastebuds
as i get ready for lunch.

for which,
i will also have poetry.
sandwiched words
that come from nowhere and everywhere, dipped in description.

for dinner, i eat poetry, too.
long free-versed
stanza-like spaghetti noodles,
filling my heart and belly with emotion.

and, for dessert,
i'll write poetry,
sweet simple lines like strawberry syrup.
a real delicate treat for readers to enjoy.

Headed towards Cathedral

perplexities of perpetual perpendicular geometry;
i don't know what it all means.
do you?
carousels of white,
leather and corduroy.
butterflies dance in the sun,
waiting to crawl back into cocoons.
bliss,
ready to be born again,
anew,
a child.
reborn in worlds so colorful,
cactus water bubbling,
perspective rising from volcanos' peaks,
chattering
with the wind's cry,
dirty sneakers and beat-up beatboxes on subway rides.
looking for the ethereal sun,
the ethereal black, white, and gray of the universe
calling us back to the womb.

lights on fireflies

mushrooms sing in rooms of white,
chiming chanting crystalizing.
hymns are discovered through touch,
enchanting enthralling—
ethereal lies in the mundane,
the dirt beneath the nails,
the nails in the box
that are the building of life...

jaded jukeboxes play the songs
of a world still developing its sound.
and when all the words have been said aloud,
new words will be created,
new lives imagined,
the mushrooms elated
at the realizations humans had,
which they journeyed through long ago.
it's all a series of rollercoasters,
galactic spirals,
ebbs and flows,
and ebbs and flows
that come and go
like lights on fireflies,
and souls that rest at night,
transported to new soils,
new lands,
new dimensions,
of varying connections,
rings on fingers and feelings that linger,
it's time for the mushrooms to sing
the song of good night.

echoes, dainty & wild

spring brings flowers, a coronation for the earth
to gather its dainty dress & lay in a field of wild.
spring brings renewal, a time of cosmic birth,
for don't you know we are all one breath, one child?
spring echoes in the minds of all who kiss the lips of time,
&, of course, fall is a culprit.
a match made beyond the heavens—the perfect partners in crime.

spring   flowers,

dainty &   wild.

a cosmic birth,

one breath,

echoes   kiss the lips

of   fall

—the perfect   crime.

Leave a message at the tone

i hear death at the door.
shovels, bells, haunts.
a fox
comes along
—invisible, adaptable—
but with keen senses,
aware of its surroundings,
saving.

intrigued,
death
postpones
his visit.

new year, cold

the winter solstice was
pandora's box.
allegations wrapped up in a pretty bow.
hesitations oozing out of
chocolate canisters.

it was realizations and eurekas too late,
but delicious lunches that left you feeling full.

the winter solstice was
chaos calmed by kiss,
lost packages found
right before the holidays.
it was tired eyes and car checks
while songs played on repeat, repeatedly
over and over and over again.

the winter solstice came,
without warning,
with only the light of the moon,
which could've been mistaken for fullness,
but we know now it's a phenomena.

it makes sense why things began with
shouts and hurrahs,
followed by shouts and goodbyes,
i love you's lingering throughout.

it was the perfect example
of the theory that
the past, present, and future
happen simultaneously,

only grabbing glimpses through the aleph,
or through the moments when reality feels
like dreams or other dimensions.

the winter solstice will come and go,
returning each year like a sea turtle to the
beach it was born,
but every time,
new happenings will be made possible in the moonlight.
and no matter the similarities,
every time will be different.

perhaps next year
the winter solstice
will bring calm instead of chaos,
peace instead of passivity,
and dreams instead of doubts.

Dakota

thank you human limitations and earthly delights
for teaching me to grow
s l o w l y,
for reminding that nothing is as instantaneous as
our timelines make them out to be.
for showing me all the many ways in which
i am moving forward
one
step
at
a
time,
towards the new beginnings
that await by the swing set,
lingering while music plays
over cardboard cutout boomboxes
that wait patiently around the corner,
just as my future awaits p a t i e n t l y for me.

thank you human limitations and earthly delights
for embracing me with sunlight,
glucose glittering my eyelids as dewdrops dance,
because deep down
i am only a plant, too.
except i am one that learned to
breathe and write and laugh and scream and be bright.
i am a complex cosmos, a galaxy within the galaxy,
a perplexing anthropomorphic mountain.
i am nature.
i am god.
i am delicious human limitations and earthly delights.

{Intentions}

Waxing Crescent

Homeostasis of the Mind

89.5 or 88.5—
temperatures or radio stations,
all one and the same,
one in the same,
ones and zeroes, ones and zeroes.
what we are is
sacred geometry,
digitized
in alien humanoid
form.
wooden chairs
of metal triangles and olives.
worn watercolor
paintings
of steel
feel
hot
under jackets of leather,
but we're accustomed
to seventy degree
homeostasis of the mind.

electric lady music

simplicity found in the intricate
is the same as
intricacies found in the simple.

it's all

                              nonsense, really.

making sense of it
is the life part.

it's the

honeycomb metal elevator,
bringing you to the horizon.

electric lady music
bringing you, beckoning you
to the ethereal.

waves

remember, everything is waves. remember, everything is waves.

life/death

to live is to live, but death is just around the corner, waiting—creaking and pacing and peaking—for the first too-errored move to come about silently, unexpectedly. but life, life is everything. it is loss and it is love. it is remorse and it is rejoice. it is death and everything else. it is all part of the cosmic equation that we call the universe, where time and space only exist on a constructed level, yet they define our realities as human beings. there's 60 seconds in one hour. 24 hours in one day. 28/30/31 days in one month. 12 months in one year. there are countless, infinite, predated years in one lifetime. then, only one question remains to be asked to the masses: how will you spend all this *time*?

spatial divinity

light shines through, always,
even through the fog,
even through the trees.
light will guide you through the moments
that make you weak at the knees.

so, let's draw rocks,
darkness-demanding or sun-scorched.
sounds, a million miles of waterfalls.
one hand hovers over the light
and we play intuition,
testing our guts,
counting the spatial divinity
between year and light-year.

canvas (on feedback loop)

the world is your canvas,

the world is your canvas,

or mix the colors with ease.

or mix the colors with ease.

paint it pretty as you please,

paint it pretty as you please,

stay between the lines,

stay between the lines,

evermore and never rotten

if i plant my feet on the ground,
can my head still be in the clouds?
growing ten feet tall like Alice,
looking at the world beyond its malice?
it's possible,
to reach a place
beyond this plane,
where the stars shine brighter
without you needing a lighter
to light the fumes you hold in your lungs.
i guess that's when the euphoria has begun
and the world's colors are no longer dull
but full
and it requires nothing
but breathing in the everything
that flows through the air,
through the wind tangled in one's hair
that presents the feeling of i *just* don't care
what everyone else is up to,
because we're all looking up at a sky that's blue.
if i shrink down to a size beyond comparison,
when i look at dawn, will i still see the horizon?
only time tells tales of times forgotten,
one where you wear your hearts on your sleeves,
evermore and never rotten.
it's okay to be lost in the thoughts
of wonderland,
but when you can come back to the present,
make sure you see what it is that *holds* your hand.

The incantation

breathe in, out / stare up at the daylight moon, pray to its goddess / for words to sync into breaths.

type rhythmically / one word at a time / the moon is my companion / my ears for words unspoken / lost among the dandelions.

past midnight, i hear her calling me to *keep writing* / *never stop writing* / to write just one more word / until the keys become a song for our ears only.

the moon ignites the incantation / even if at times i have no idea it is her behind the muse / *as long as you write with intention*, she tells me / and i do.

i do nothing but listen / listen to the sounds she crashes onto dusk waves / listen to the cicadas in summer sing / listen to the wolf's howl at the *moon over bourbon street* / i listen closely enough / to hear my own heartbeat writing poetry.

and then, all i have to do is transform its form / to one that sticks to paper.

{Reflection}

> *"The Moon is the reflection of your heart,*
> *and moonlight is the twinkle of your love."*
> — **Debasish Mridha**

Full Quarter

Clocks ring nine

the ants eat the bee,
translocating it to somewhere else on the counter,
too many little legs to count just how many
there are.

nature can be cruel, however
never asking for more.
new days shine lights on
necessities that, to us humans, seem impure.

the little bee is gone now,
the only
traces are the remaining ants
that suckle the counter for remnants.

scattered, yet collected,
some crawl towards me too,
sadly, i'm too big of a tasty meal.
shoo at them i do.

clocks ring nine while the sun
cloaks the sky with its heat and light,
carrying on until the settling night
sneaks up on us, too,
to start everything again tomorrow.

white satin silk

she spent *nights in white satin*,
or was it silk
that embodied her body in warmth?

she caressed herself
into her cocoon
of chipped chai, chained,

ever unknowing
if she would emerge
a stunning image of more than just beautiful silk.

poets read poetry

poets read poetry,
their own poems
pending in their minds.

Lyrical lady

crystals hang from her ears
in jewelry drenched in silver and gold.
her never-brushed hair is
only knotted when kissed
by the winds of everyday.
she sits to read her mary oliver
in her peek-a-boo socks and imagines
that one day she'll awake humming
a tune of peace and delight in
a home of her own—and somewhere
near or far away,
someone will sit reading their own little poet
in peek-a-boo socks.

she picks up a note-
book and quill
and transcribes a poem,
a lyric,
a verse,
a song,
wiggling her unpainted toes
to the music only playing in
her head
and dreams of pumpkin bread
and the returning autumn,
because with it comes change
and she's ready for her recognition.

spirals of sound

it's a different dynamic,
but i'm still in the same place,
silenced by the spirals of sounds
that escape the faces and basses
of those around me.

when will time tell a tale
of a life lived free?

mortal nesting dolls at midnight twilight

i like to think that
at least i know
the universe knows
exactly what it's doing.
every critique, kiss, calculated beyond cusps
of pure randomness.

i like to think
the universe had me download this delicacy
just for you, listener, fellow poet, writer, reader, creative dreamer
to bask in,
as we all connect to cosmic consciousness.

i like to think that
everything will wonderfully work itself out,
though there's a creeping doubt
that sometimes sits
on the lightless hours of night,
the pitch black crickets chirping starryless light, pollution
that sometimes waits in the
"already tomorrow, but i'm not asleep" midnight twilight.

but there's a melody to the frogs' croaks,
a song of different pitches presented to different ears,
some annoyed and some grown to enjoy the
sweet-wet, sweat-wet summer.

the birds that sing soft symphonies as the sun rises
are my favorite,
in those hours where slowly the light seeps in
through the blinds and suddenly the room feels alive,
painted anew by the rays of new days, new possibilities.

{Change}

Waxing Gibbous

for change is not foreboding / on the intergalactic cosmo-way

hello, my darling,
do not fear, do not fret.

you have entered
into the intergalactic cosmo-way.

please,
keep your light-orbed hands and feet

within your bodily fleshy vessel
and enjoy the life-journey ride.

for change is not foreboding,
if you look through *brand new eyes*.

and i hope this evolution never ceases

i am ever-evolving,
layers of hair, skin, sweat shed,
morphing from moth to moth, butterfly to butterfly.

i see it through old photographs,
the changes in my hair, my body.
the changes in my smile, my style.

i see the growth in my tastes,
like sands wrapped in waves,
like literature, a friend i hold dear, ever-changing genres.

tides pull back and forth to reveal
variations of my soul,
all different phases with the same face, slightly more old,

and i hope that this evolution never ceases,
that even when i am nothing but dirt and bones
i am continuing to evolve and change and grow.

perhaps in another lifetime,
perhaps in another lifeline.

metamorphosis

we learn
metamorphosis
without ever
shedding our skin.

strange behavior

habits are built,
for better or worse.
smoke-filling lungs,
the taste of rum,
going to be early & waking up early.
changing the routine,
changing our minds,
thoughts coming undone
in the whispers of night.
train stations & car rides,
taking us any place,
all those scenes without care.

but those habits
might come back like ghosts & ghouls.
for the bad ones stay in theirs caves
& the good ones rise like the sun at your back,
casting shadows into the heavens.
& to that, let us toast.
after all, isn't just
being alive—being aware that you're alive,
the chances of consciousness in the vastness of space & time—
strange behavior?

Peeling

sprinkled
on the bathroom floor
is skin confetti
from my sheddings,
my layers becoming undone.

life changes like tides,
making ways and waves for
new beginnings
whose outcomes are still
unknown.

unconsciously cocooned,
now metamorphosing
into something new and true,
peeling off onion layers
that may or may not water the eyes.

sprinkled
on the bathroom floor
is skin confetti
from my sheddings
and i'm ready
for what's to come.

Continually evolving

i can be an impatient little thing,
annoyed at the growth i
begged so long for
simply because
it is not the end goal.

i can be a heart-full thing,
finding love and lust
in every breath,
raindrop kiss,
& tired eyes of maraschino bliss.

i can be a half-girl thing,
holding on to that childhood innocence
i left behind ages ago,
on a climbed tree,
on my first blood-stain.

i am an all woman thing now
& i will embrace her curves;
the one that taught me to dream
& sing & recite poetry,
the one that holds me in tender arms
when i'm being a half-girl thing;
the one that is one with all
when i'm being a heart-full thing;
and the one that pushes my head in the
water of reflection and rains gratitude upon
on my impatient little thing.

i am all faces.
i am all phases,

kissed sweetly under blue clouds
while gray skies watch from stars' peaks.

yellow brick roses

she rode in
on yellow brick roses,
gold adorning her fiery head.
and when the
gates of heaven opened,
everyone gasped and stared to no end.

she kissed the
foreheads of sinners,
beggars who had never seen bliss.
and from beneath
her folds of silk skirts,
you could hear a snake's faint hiss.

her walk was
elegant,
never a step out of place.
and her smile
was wild, beautiful enough
to transcend all of space.

as she entered,
she left the town
a more beautiful ruin than before.
and she altered
the chaotic cosmos
by opening the daisy-chained door.

communication is a trojan horse

communication is a trojan horse,
pandora's box,
a trapdoor
that can be opened
from either side.

a ticking time bomb,
a honey comb,
sweetening the world.
or pepper spray,
aimed at the eyes,
leaving a
lingering
bitter taste,
bittersweet taste,
at the back of the throat.

an onion of
a nesting doll,
layered with double entendres,
sticky like syrup,
savored,
left behind
on the tongue,
and an aroma that remains
tacked like taffy,
like a fly on the wall.

is it better to keep silent
or communicate it all?

{Soul Promises}

Full Moon

looking at the world as a child seeing fractals of light

a child cries, but only on the inside;
the adult she is now has become weathered.
if only she'd recognize she's on her own side
and they could live in this fairytale together,
a place where flowers are never dried
and no soul on the earth has ever lied.

a euphoric vision of mystical paradise
with dancing beings full of light,
limited to only the awakened eyes,
who within and without can't help but shine bright
through the fields of hills, green, and blue skies.
yes, here is where imagination lies.

to have faith is to believe in the unknown,
and while that may seem difficult,
even while one has grown,
if you believe in it enough, you'll see the result
and travel to the land where flowers have flown,
where, in the rivers, lie miles of colorful stone.

a sky full of clouds is still a sky so blue
and here, no happiness or love or light can be taken.
to look at the world through fractals is new,
but it's always been there waiting for you to awaken.
it's something she saw before she grew,
but now she remembers the magic that got her through.

the child did not lose her sense of wonder,
for it has always lied beneath her freckled skin

and, grown, she found joy in the sounds of thunder.
she trusted herself and breathed it all in,
for as above is the same as down under,
where flowers and the weeds would never surrender.

a moth fell in love with the moon
(& the enamoured moon blushes with love)

on a cool moonlit night,
as cicadas and crickets began their chirps,
a moth looked up to the heavenly skies
and fell deeply in love with the moon and her curves:

oh my! what brightness!
love of my life, you are
sweeter than honey on my hands and feet,
feet and wings i wish i could extend into the cosmos
to offer you my loving embrace...

nonsense,
my dear!
you are effervescent.
how i long to kiss your craters...

the sun is rising,
but you are whom i seek.
forget me not, true love...

until we meet again, my sweet.
to the moon and back...

Full Moon

i hear your love-spelled words, but,
alas, i cannot see you.
you are mistaken, my love,
my brightness is only borrowed...

darling,
you turn me scarlet,
but the sun is rising
and i must bid you adieu...

i'll hold you forever in memory,
to the moon and back...

kisses on the shoreline

like the ocean's shore,
wave after wave,
the tide may come to kiss me sweetly
or leave me dry;
the tide may drown my world
or stay with me when i cry.

each speck of sand
is an experience,
an emotion,
a thought,
a burst,
but i will remain,
strong, more resilient
than if i were to let myself rot.

like the ocean's shore,
wave after wave,
crash after crash,
i will remain
until my body turns to ash.

and even then,
i will still be here,
a part of this universe
that loves me
and i love, too,
so dear.

symphonic stories for melodic muses

on one hand,
i have
beats and licks,
kicks and drums,
that syncopate the symphonies
and melodies
that lyrically run races
through my mind.

on the other hand,
i have
pages and paper cuts,
letters and words,
that lose themselves in the wind,
sometimes finding
themselves
on handwritten
or type-texted
notes.

i balance
with ease
(or so i like to tell myself),
letting the muses come and go
as they please,
as they introduce
themselves.

we're smitten with each other;
one creative cut in two,
cut from the same cloth,
a happily ever after, after all.

an old god's nostalgia

a new light enters the horizon.
the waves embrace the sand
in a waterfall kiss.
they meet and mingle,
but only for a second.
as roaches are killed,
couples lay in stars,
cities blaze in distant utopias,
fingers caress thumbs,
teeth hurt,
and in the distance,
ship lights burn.

the ocean swallows
whole
all the thoughts of the day,
encompassing the night
in a melodic sway,
a hum of a tune.
people walk
like seagulls
avoiding crashes,
but hungry
for what could lie
in the maybe,
in the unknown.
the tickles of time
remembered,
then forgotten.

tonight,
the sky is
illuminated
by an old god's
nostalgia.

Sen Qaydan Bilasan (how do you know)

eucalyptus armpits and plum pants.
acres of trees, skinny and green.
somewhere on the other side of the world,
there's a guitar playing 80s uzbekistan
on the radio waves
that transmit invisibly
onto canvases of sound.

yellow flowers match signs:
a message of the divine,
connection between
the here, the now,
the gone, the tethered,
the vibrations
of the synth and the sun
all combining to form one.

Limbs

my body aches.
limb to limb,
pulled and stretched
across the cosmos.

is it too bad to give too much?

to give
and give
and give
until your heart grows
three times three sizes.
until you're filled
with love
because you're spreading
l-o-v-e, love.

my body aches,
tingles
from the magic in my veins
and god knows

i'll give
and give
and give
all the love, hope, and magic
that courses through me
because i have enough
to give.

to myself,
to others,

from
limb

        to

                  limb.

On Love

my love for writing poetry
is a hummingbird drinking
the sweetest nectar,
a wild fire that can't be
tamed, but tames itself,
cereal left to sog in a bowl.

my love for writing poetry
is the July sun,
a library of used books
that smell ripe,
the blood that courses
my veins
while mycelium courses
the ground.

my love for writing poetry
is a New York New Year's kiss,
mistakes made on a typewriter
that make the text look
prettier, more real.

my love for writing poetry
is a fire-breathing dragon,
guava and cream cheese,
dreams on dreams on dreams.

my love for writing poetry
is a sweet nothing
that speaks of everything.

{Gratitude}

> *"With freedom, books, flowers, and the Moon,*
> *who could not be happy?"*
> — Oscar Wilde

Waning Gibbous

Designed by the tide

the sun
glitters
on the water
like diamonds.
iridescent skin,
warm salty milk of a
breast
and the rest
is history,
a mystery
of how we got here;
texting thumbs
and comfortable numb-
ness, a universe bliss,
a message of untethered,
a serenity
that swallows the vastness
and cools the mind.
lingering pesky isms of the eye
create clouds of pearly white,
dancing to a sound designed by the tide.

Moon magicians

subway tunnels and brown-bagged booze,
we head our separate ways, feeding off the aura blues.

walking the streets of the city of lights,
a glaze of starry nights
left dangling in our eyes.

we followed the music through back alleyways,
arriving at the same station, awaiting different trains,

standing, a railway track apart.
i don't know you by story but i know you by heart;
moon magicians, cloaks and coats painted in art.

we slowly vanish back like we're only mere mortals,
through the cracks in the rides, we slip into our portals.

back to our worlds, our realities,
a combination of vanilla, cinnamon, and always summer breeze.
until next time,
oh, please,
let us never forget the new york in august festivities.

Ophelia

if Ophelia could see
how many songs
have been written
about her,
how many artists
she has inspired,
she would smile,
amused in her grave,
content
that somehow,
some way,
she found her way
to make a difference.

For my mother and father, the unifying cluster of stars that made a sun

this one is for the ones who made me,
the ones who gave me
everything they had—
the good, the bad,
the in between.
the two
who fused
themselves
to form
me.
for without their love,
their support,
i wouldn't be here
breaking bread
with all who come across
my words.

summer skies smile upon us when kissed by raindrops

the blues and hues of orange
blend together so nicely against the sun's rays.
a rainbow of muted colors is
against the backdrop of rain.
it's a painting of us by something
higher than us,
something unexplainable.
but isn't it more wonderful
to call it magic?
and simply not believe your eyes
at this divine existence,
the love song
between us and summer skies.

we'll always have boba to feel closer together

we bond over boba,
slippery tapioca pearls
filling the holes of time,
slipping into sticky sunday, mundane afternoons,
making us whole again
one smooth sip at a time.
we'll see each other soon enough,
trading our boba cups,
letting the desert dessert drink
melt us into the traveling sun.
like brown sugar drip,
we'll fall into stride,
sugary and child-like,
regardless of passed time.

the MET

there's something about *you*. something about the grandness of it all. the mesh between art & history that reigns past constructs of time, space, religion, & all else. the emotions that are bottled into a single painting, a panting piece of art, preserved for centuries, centennials. for new generations to uncover and ponder upon.

Autumnal moon

i smell of pumpkin bread
and white chocolate chips,
but it is still summer
so i can't bring out
the orange hues and apple pies.

my favorite season, only
a breath away,
lingers in the corners
of my mind.
i wait for her like dried rosebuds
await the spring,
like cubs await the first licks of melted snow—
the sun's reflection through trees
on the ground.

i smell the pumpkin bread on my fingers,
beneath my nail beds and dream of
daisies, calendulas, and the
sweet smell of cinnamon,
ripe with want.
it's fruition for the autumnal feast
at the end of the season.

i wish i could host it, bring it closer.
melted candles sticking to mantles,
glasses drunk off sweet strawberry wine,
laughs ricocheting off the forest leaves,
barefoot dancing in the dirt and moonlight,
caught in its spotlight,
listening
to the witch's song and howl

that blows out the light but does not leave us
in the dark,
for we are forever accompanied
by the autumnal moon.

i return to the present—
the year does not matter,
for it is all the same days living different moments.
the summer clouds, sun, and skies
call me from the window
and i finish my love letter to the fall
and fall in love with the remnants of summer.

.

Waning Gibbous

{Forgiveness}

Third Quarter

tenacity paints the black and white alchemy

devils dress in white with angel wings,
smoke following every step they take,
leaving prisms of spirals.
they touch leafy grounds of gold,
turning tourmaline to sapphire,
combining and collapsing all things
into one dimension of crystal and metal.

devils are angels in disguise,
tethered to one another,
living beneath the stairs
that lead to grounds of heavens,
intertwined like *buried alchemy*.

the night sky
kisses the sun's eyes
and the big ball of gas blushes
at a lovely moon,
a cheekbone
of pure warmth,
and somewhere,
a devil—
or perhaps an angel?—
is holding
a golden heart-shaped bow.

moon dust

ruler of the skies,
you are but merely moon dust
in a child's eyes.

there are rotten raisin grapes in my gut

and i want to scream,
break the wineglass,
so it shatters like spirits.

i've lost my voice,
left it on the dinner table
with the words we swore at each other,
and i wish i could take them back,
wish i would have swallowed my tongue or just drank the damned wine

but as pain pulls
tight in my chest like an accordion,
you're already over it.
apology accepted
before the words could escape either of our crimson mouths.

French music reminds me of a higher self that has just lost subjective identity

the death of ego
evokes community.
a relationship with god: the self,
the materialistic world becomes
mundane
as you begin to focus on spirit.

the death of ego
evokes realization:
all self-doubts and judgements
were not coming from within.
no. instead, they were coming from without.

even now, after everything

if you look closely,
you'll come to notice that
everything has a pattern.
the universe itself
moves in spirals
of chaos and order
and all in between.
we come and go from this earth
like water,
falling like rain,
rising up, evaporating until it's time
to fall again.
and we continue this cyclical lifestyle,
unknown to most of us,
scared to die,
scared of the unknown and what's to come.
we are a species with a memory problem,
forgetting our greatness,
our grandness,
forgetting that we, in fact, know and hold
the keys to the universe.
but we forget
when we reduce ourselves
to the beings we are now,
full of self and senses.
but when it is our time again
to leave this realm,
some of us glad
and some of us sad,
we'll miss this earth
and all its chaos and beauty.

and you may scoff,
"miss earth, you say,
even now, after everything?"
and the answer is yes,
because there's always so much
to learn
from this water-filled planet
floating through the vastness
of space.
there's simply too much too learn,
too much for just one lifetime.
so, yes,
even now, after everything,
i choose to wake up,
grateful, giddy
that i get to see another day of
the wind flirting with the trees,
the hot ball of gas that brings to life the light
to participate in festivities,
technologies and synchronicities,
nostalgia and societal intricacies,
e v e r y t h i n g.
because there will come a day
when it is all gone,
our generation
far beyond,
and it would pang and pain
at my heart
if the earth didn't know
just how much we loved.

Vanitas

there's   never enough of it,
but sometimes,   there's too much.
its taste lingers   on my tongue.
though i've never felt its   texture.
it's here and it's not and i wonder
how it passes,   how it allows healing
to penetrate   the broken corners of my bones,
the scabbed edges of my skin,
the knife-wounded hollows   of my heart.
it tickles   my senses,
reminding me,   silently,   of my breath,
that i am alive   in this form,
in this lifetime,
for only   a cycle of stars.

In the labyrinth is a cherry tree, and there, an old god rests and reminds you of your endeavors

money trees lie untainted, untamed
in the depths of the labyrinths that are
the universe for those willing to try.

blessings and lessons disguised as
masked muses for the persevering to
unravel, unwrap.

money grows on the backs of those who
lack the endurance,
in the hands of those who push
                       on and

                                    on and

                                                on.

through downfalls
and pits of despair,
lazy sundays,
pots of gold hiding beneath
seemingly infinite stairs.

where there's a will, the way is soon to come,
like a baby who learns to stop
salivating on its thumb,
like a bird who refuses to fear the heights of flying.

there's so much out in the roads,
both less traveled and trafficked.

beyond the crashing waves,
there's a sandbar that leads to
walking with god.

money trees spring like cherry blossoms
under masks of sunday morning sunrays,
blinded or glassed off,
under surreal leaves that believe
in power of will and focus
                              an d foc u s
                                    and f o c u s .
never stop riding the wind's compass,
it's strapped-saddle will.
one day less to the
tower of gold
made of arteries,
hearts on fleek,
reserved for those not planning to deceive.

.

a tiger is a kind of cat

emotions are wild beasts,
cutting through you
like a hot knife cuts through butter,
and you lie in the haze of a
sentimental tug of war.

i have lived
at least
nine lives,
i have earned
my tigris
stripes.

and each new patch of pattern
is an emotion felt;
a white spot behind the ears,
like hearts on sleeves;
an expanse of underbelly,
reserved for moments serene.
each strike earns me a stripe
and my heart is building up
its armor like flowers
build their petals.

i know now i am a cat that will
never be domesticated.

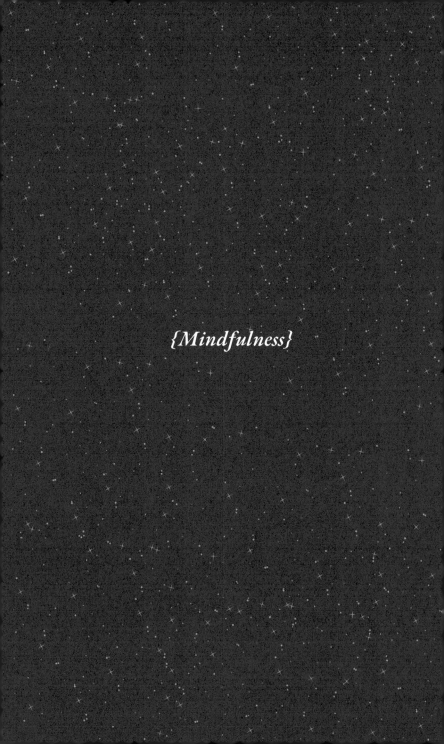

{Mindfulness}

Waning Crescent

spontaneous rest stops at cocoa beach

sun on my back,
ice touching toes.
who knew the waves could be so poetic,
so shocking,
so sure?
who knew the ocean could be so enticing?
you. i love.
birds flying,
flapping,
planes hovering—
unidentified flying objects
to time travelers
coming into the future,
our present,
under steampunk glasses,
not rose-colored—
where salty, sandy toes
may as well be grains of flour
sticking to sticky sweaty skin
that loves the flow of the breeze
the body alerts daintily.
the birds search in hunger for food
as the waves ebb and flow,
rise and crash
against shorelines
of ash-ridden specks.
a staircase of clouds
leads nowhere but blue,
a dissimilar blue to the water,
a rippled concoction of curiosity
typed on a phone

as the crashing tides
design the type.
a sudden silence of words stops on the tongue,
streams lay still
and epiphanies are had.
and in the end,
one breathes in the unscented air,
the eyes close,
only to see the sun's red reflected from
memory
and realize
all art is art as we are all art.
lives put to pen, paper, phones.
one day here, next gone like ghosts
but never forgotten
in the infinite eyes of the cosmos.
the universe keeps record of the many ways
to live,
the many ways one could live
and life could form more life.
lost to some souls and found in others
as birds almost pick at feet,
black and white feathers calm in the rustle.

memories play like music when left to their own devices

i don't want to forget
and yet, i am bound.
for there are countless <moments>
in a lifetime to experience.
countless <sunrises>
to bring in morning warmth.
countless <smiles>
to make the <heart> feel whole.

i want to remember every single person who believed in me,
even if their time in my life was
counted like school bells counting off days until summer.
i want to remember the messages the angels sent
through their infinities and infinite eyes
that i first deemed coincidence.
i want to remember every single white hair
in my father's beard,
how it was before the gray and stubble.
i want to remember my mother's sweet embrace,
how her fingers were always cool to the touch against my skin
and mentioned every time.
i want to remember my sister's laughter,
the way her smile shined like a diamond
in the blue-hued mountainous skylight.
i want to remember the first time a creative endeavor
connected me to those who needed
somebody to love
and we all felt the light.

tu-tum / tu-tump

i fall asleep   *tu-tum / tu-tump*
to my heartbeat,   *tu-tum / tu-tump*
my constant reminder   *tu-tum / tu-tump*
that i am alive.   *tu-tum / tu-tump*

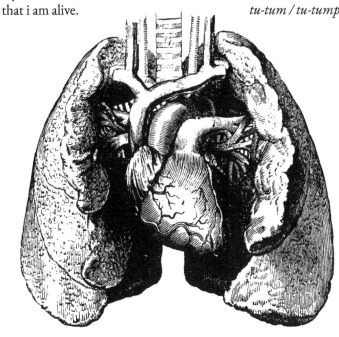

tears for fears

everybody wants to rule the world

but, i just want to live in it.
bask in the breeze
that makes my skin goose up,
taste euphoria on my tongue,
lick the icing off of cupcakes of raspberry,
making blasphemous statements,
like shouting
i love you!
across the universe,
amidst a meadow's mist.
and i'll join the trees, the bees
in their nakedness,
and together,
we'll wash away the
tears for fears that
stained our cheeks,
like new york on midnight's eve,
new orleans's bourbon street,
stripped down naked ninth circle rawness.
we'll wash away the
days before we lived
in mindfulness,
never forgetting what it taught us.

minutes, moments, nursery rhymes

time is nonlinear—

past, present, future

all occurring at once—

triplets of the same kind

at the same time—

minutes, moments, nursery rhymes

sometimes all too much
for our overwhelmed brains to
really fathom and touch.

time is nonlinear,
but we don't see it that way.
yet, maybe one day,
that concept will cusp on change,
because all there is
is death and rebirth—

infinite timelines

to experience on earth.

white rabbit

come and find me.
fall through the rabbit hole,
find your own wonderland.
awaken to the cheshire moon,
the caterpillar's smoke.
you may be surprised at what the dormouse said,
but when you awake in your own bed,
the sunlight's kiss
shyly peeking
through the blinds,
and there's a raven on a writing desk
asking why a raven is a like a writing desk,
remember,
it wasn't a dream at all.

Utopia lies in the place of mystic bees

utopia lies in the place of mystic bees,
off the endangered species list,
drunk off wildflowers & peonies,
pollinating the world with their kiss.
if only they could understand
the fate of the world lies in their hands.

utopia lies in outstanding connection,
in understanding one another's perspective,
greeting an unknown hand with affection,
allowing the ego to dissolve subjective-
thoughts, even if, at first, only on the deepest inside.
soon, they will realize they are more than just their minds.

utopia lies in the war on nuclear war,
a truce between all nations to finally occur,
closing off the battle lines, the blood-stained, wretched door,
returning to the days of paradise, where we were in *some* before.
if we can understand each other, we can survive,
if we can connect on a spiritual level, we can thrive.

utopia lies in the realization that we are all one universe,
one interconnectedness of experiences told through a different lense,
a sweet song of symphonies, a hymn of only one verse,
blasted on beaten boomboxes held up to the sky in attempt of a cleanse.
it was once known long ago by those in the temples of time.
it is known by those now who are making the spiritual climb.

utopia lies at the edge of our galaxy,
but to the ones thinking in ego, in dystopia,
a world of peace and balance is blasphemy,
a subconscious choosing of myopia,

where imagination & love seem to be faint,
& the touching hands & hearts only miraculously free of taint.

utopia lies in understanding, in the sharing of prose,
where one takes words on the page & opens hearts to changes of pace,
tending to the thorned garden, where produced is a single red rose.
& we realize we are all *one,* coming in for an overdue embrace.
if only today's message told stories of chaos, order, the marital cosmos;
we would finally learn to hold each other dearly & oh so close.

sin stuck, sweet love

forgive me, self,
for i have sinned.
i have not written in days,
a poem, that is.
though not for lack of trying.
you see, i had been stuck.
the words had not come.
there had been no
cosmic download
of what it was
i was wanting to write
in prose.

forgive me,
for i have sinned
and since not written,
yet i call myself a writer,
a poet, that is.

i have cheated my own poetry,
focusing on fiction,
yet do not dare claim
i love one more than another.
how does a mother
choose between two children?
simple. she doesn't.

consider this my public display of affection,
of apology,
to you, my sweet child.
you are not forgotten,
you are not abandoned,

you are simply resting
while i put the house in order.
i am tending to your sister,
who is merely an infant
while you—this book—are close
to leaving the nest.
forgive me, child,
if i have lost touch,
but please know that i
will always love you so much.

while i will hold a place
for my novel-writing,
my poetry will always be
my first love.

.

Waning Crescent

Notes

- The poem *echoes, dainty & wild* was inspired by Tova Greene's poem *echo*, from her collection, *ohso: poems about love & other matters that are nearly ohso close.*

- In the poem *new year, cold*, the word "aleph" is to be defined by Paulo Coelho's definition from his book *Aleph*: "In Borges' story, the Aleph is a point in space that contains all other points. Anyone who gazes into it can see everything in the universe from every angle."

- There are a couple of poems in this collection that refer to Lewis Carroll's *Alice's Adventures in Wonderland* and *Through The Looking Glass: evermore and never rotten* and *white rabbit.*

- The poem *Dakota* is for Lady Dakota Warren, and was inspired by her use of the phrase, "thank you human limitations and early delights."

- The poem *canvas (on feedback loop)* was inspired by Katie Scruggs Galloway's poem *Window Eleven // Feedback Loop* from *Still, and Still Moving.*

- In *The incantation*, which was inspired by Kirk Hammett's *The Incantation*, the phrase "*moon over bourbon street*" is from Sting's *Moon Over Bourbon Street.*

- In *white satin silk*, the phrase "*nights in white satin*" is from The Moody Blues's *Nights in White Satin.*

- *looking at the world as a child seeing fractals of light* was an NSU Creative Writing project, with some new edits, of course. I hope I'm making you proud, Professor Friedman.

- The phrase "*the enamoured moon blushes with love*" in the title piece poem is a direct quote from Edgar Allan Poe's poem *Israfel.*

- The poem *Sen Qaydan Bilasan (how do you know)* was inspired by a lengthy carride and the song *Sen Qaydan Bilasan* by Davron G'oyipov, which I have yet to find and listen to again.

- The poem *On Love* was inspired by Charles Bukowski's poetry collection *On Love*.

- *Moon magicians* is for Pucci, Vicky, Franchy, and Aldo.
                    Thank you all for making New York City more magical.

- *For my mother and father, the unifying cluster of stars that made a sun* is clearly a poem for my parents, whom I love dearly. Thank you for your constant support.
                                            Los adoro.

- *the MET* is an ode to the Metropolitan Museum of Art, which, along with New York City as a whole, will always hold space in my heart.

- *we'll always have boba to feel closer together* is for my sister, Yaima.
                                    I love you, Tata.

- The phrase *"buried alchemy"* in *tenacity paints the black and white alchemy* comes from Covisky's *Buried Alchemy*.

- The line *"hearts on fleek"* in the poem *In the labyrinth is a cherry tree, and there, an old god rests and reminds you to focus on your endeavors* is a direct quote from Lana Del Rey's poem *Sugarfish* in *Violet Bent Backwards over the Grass*.

- *a tiger is a kind of cat* was inspired by Laura Leezy and Khruangbin's *Connaissais de Face*.

- *tears for fears* was inspired by *Everybody Wants to Rule the World* by Tears for Fears.

Notes & Acknolwedgments

- *Utopia lies in the place of mystic bees* was originally submitted to the Jericho Fellowship.

- *sin stuck, sweet love* is a very special piece, and clearly, you can interpret why. I look forward to sharing with you what is to come.

Okay, enough notes.

There are two people whom I want to thank heavily for helping me bring this book to fruition:
Kim Rashidi & Athena Edwards
Kimmy, I'm forever grateful for your help on making this book what it is. I will always be reminded of you on Sundays.
Athena, thank you for reading thoroughly through these pieces and providing your literary eye. I'm so grateful for Digressions just because I got to meet you.
Of course, I want to thank my parents for their continuous support, always. As well as my sister for always believing in me.
Thank you all for all you do.
I also want to give a special thanks to Aldo Leon and Giuseppe Storniolo for pushing me to experiment with my poetry and encouraging me to let it grow and evolve as I grow and evolve.
Aldo, thank you for always pushing me to keep writing and to always put my writing first. You have my heart.
I want to thank Vintage Illustrations for adding a little more flair to this work of art and providing something extra to the eye.
I also want to thank Nathalie Zarza for my author photo.
To Indie Earth Publishing, thank you for being a blessing.
I want to give a special thank you to all of the authors who have supported *A Moth Fell In Love With The Moon*:
Kimmy, Kendall, Cheyenne, Joey, Salem, Erin.

Lastly, and perhaps most importantly,
I want to thank *you*, Reader,
for without you, I would not be able to achieve my dreams.
May this book be an inspiration for you to pursue yours.

About the Author

© Nathalie Zarza

Flor Ana is a Cuban-American writer, poet, and musician who made her literary debut with her self-published poetry collection, *Perspective (and other poems),* which went on to become a bestseller at Barnes & Noble locations across South Florida. Since her literary debut, Flor has released various poetry collections, including *The Language of Fungi & Flowers* and *Nourish Your Temple: Self-Love & Care Poetry. A Moth Fell In Love With The Moon* is her fourth collection.

As of this writing, Flor is working on her debut novel, and hopes to dive into the world of fiction writing. Always a lover of academics, Flor obtained a Journalism degree at Nova Southeastern University, where she also minored in English Literature and Marketing, and was the copy editor of the school newspaper, The Current. When Flor is not spending time in the literary world, she enjoys performing with her band Leather & Lace, listening to music, reading, cooking, spending time with her loved ones, and being out in nature.

Connect with Flor:
Instagram: @littleearthflower

About the Publisher

INDIE EARTH

PUBLISHING

Indie Earth Publishing is an independent,
author-first co-publishing company based in Miami, FL, dedicated to
giving writers the creative freedom they deserve when
publishing their poetry, fiction, and short story collections. Indie Earth
provides its authors a plethora of services meant to aid them in their
book publishing experiences and finally feel they are releasing the book
of their dreams.

With Indie Earth Publishing, you are more than just an author, you are
part of the Indie Earth creative family,
making a difference one book at a time.

www.indieearthbooks.com

For inquiries, please email:
indieearthpublishinghouse@gmail.com

Instagram: @indieearthbooks

Ingram Content Group UK Ltd.
Milton Keynes UK
UKHW020854280423
420925UK00009B/95

9 798986 989150